D0723089

Harp Seals

Harp Seals

by Olga Cossi

A Carolrhoda Nature Watch Book

 Carolrhoda Books, Inc./Minneapolis

Text copyright © 1991 by Olga Cossi

All rights reserved. International copyright secured. No part of this book may be reproduced, stored in a retrieval system, or transmitted in any form or by any means, electronic, mechanical, photocopying, recording, or otherwise, without the prior written permission of the Publisher except for the inclusion of brief quotations in an acknowledged review.

This book is available in two editions:
Library binding by Carolrhoda Books, Inc.
Soft cover by First Avenue Editions
241 First Avenue North
Minneapolis, MN 55401

LIBRARY OF CONGRESS CATALOGING-IN-PUBLICATION DATA

Cossi, Olga.
    Harp seals / by Olga Cossi
        p.   cm.
    "A Carolrhoda nature watch book."
    Includes index.
    Summary: Describes the life cycle, migratory patterns, behavior, and habitat of the harp seal.
    ISBN 0-87614-437-7 (lib. bdg.)   ISBN 0-87614-567-5 (pbk.)
    1. Harp seal—Juvenile literature. [1. Harp seal. 2. Seals (Animals)]   I. Title.
QL737.P64C67   1991   90-2481
599.74′8—dc20   CIP

Manufactured in the United States of America

2   3   4   5   6   7   8   9   10   00   99   98   97   96   95   94   93

To Don, my husband and friend, for his gracious support of my love for animals.

Special thanks to Dr. Graham Worthy, Department of Marine Biology at Texas A & M University; Dr. Donald B. Siniff, Department of Ecology and Behavioral Biology at the University of Minnesota; Ted Crail, Creative Services Director for the Animal Protection Institute of America; Vivia Boe, former Greenpeace International Seal Campaign Coordinator; Barry MacKay, Wildlife Coordinator for the Toronto Humane Society; and Vanessa Gwynne for their assistance in the preparation of this book.

Photographs courtesy of: front cover, pp. 2, 3, 4-5, 6, 8-9, 11, 12, 13, 20, 22 (left), 23, 26 (top and bottom), 28 (top and bottom), 29, 31, 32, 33 (top and bottom), 34, 35 (bottom), 36 (top and bottom), 37, 38 (top and bottom), 39, 40-41, 42, Kit M. Kovacs; pp. 7, 16-17, 22 (right), 25 (bottom), 27, 30, 35 (top), 43, 44-45, back cover, Kathy Strain/Animal Protection Institute; pp. 10, 14, 15, International Fund for Animal Welfare; pp. 24, 25 (top), David Rinehart/Photography 501(c)(3)

front cover: *This harp seal pup, called a yellowcoat, is about two days old.*

back cover: *A beater peeks through a lead.*

A bird's-eye view of female harp seals on the ice

In the north Atlantic Ocean, where crusty ice covers much of the water, harp seals gather to give birth to their pups. Except for the once-a-year events of pupping and shedding, harp seals rarely come out of the water. But for now, the harp seal herd's winter migration has ended, and the female seals take to the ice.

6

Harp seal pups are covered with long white fur, while adult harp seals can be identified by the black markings on their backs.

Harp seals are easy to identify. The pups are known for their silky white fur, and the adults can be recognized by their outstanding markings. The adults have sleek black heads and an unusual black design across their silvery gray shoulders and backs. The design looks somewhat like a harp or a saddle and gives them their name, harp seal, and their nickname, saddleback.

Like all young mammals, harp seal pups drink their mother's milk for nourishment.

Harp seals are true seals with the scientific name of *Phoca groenlandica*, meaning "the Greenland seal." There is, however, some disagreement over this classification—some scientists classify harp seals as *Pagophilus groenlandicus*, meaning "the ice lover from Greenland." Although they live mainly in the water, harp seals are **mammals**. Mammals breathe air, give birth to their young (rather than laying eggs), and the females produce milk from their mammary glands to feed their young. Harp seals are similar to other species of seal, but they have unique physical characteristics and a lifestyle of their own.

Right: *An underwater view of a harp seal, showing off its webbed flippers*

Opposite: *Back flippers are used to thrust harp seals out of the water, but harp seals also use their front claws to grip the ice in their effort to haul out of the water.*

Like all other seals, sea lions, and walruses, harp seals are **pinnipeds**, or feather-footed animals, with flippers instead of hands and feet. The front flippers are shorter and smaller than the back flippers and are located on either side of a seal's long body. They are used mainly to pull the heavy harp seal across ice. Each front flipper has five webbed fingers with long, sharp claws that are useful for clinging onto and scratching holes through ice.

The back flippers, and a short tail, stick straight out in back of a harp seal as a continuation of its body. Each back flipper has five long toes enclosed in its webbing. The toes are spread apart to give the seal tremendous thrust, speed, and power while swimming.

An adult harp seal is an excellent swimmer and can reach a racing speed of 15 mph (24 kph). The muscular flex of the back flippers makes possible the sudden turns and deep dives for which harp seals are noted. The back flippers enable harps to haul out of the water onto the ice. Hauling out is a clumsy movement—part leap, part lunge, and part glide. By contrast, when they are in the water, harp seals are excellent swimmers whose motions are smooth, swift, and graceful.

One reason harp seals perform so well in the water is that their powerful bodies are shaped like torpedoes that are covered with fur. The fur is lined with a thick layer of fat, called **blubber**, which shuts in body heat and shuts out the deadly chill of the icy seas these seals inhabit.

A school of harp seals swimming in icy water

Taking time out for a relaxing backstroke

Adult male and female harp seals are about the same size, the females being only slightly smaller. In prime condition, an adult weighs about 300 pounds (130 kg) and is about 6 feet (1.80 m) long.

Groups of up to 10 adult harp seals form individual schools. Hundreds of thousands of such schools make up a herd. Each group moves together within a herd in a living wave of streamlined bodies swimming through brilliant blue waters. The harps dive, leap, and swim at the water's surface. They race and bob in and out of holes in the ice, called **leads**. Harp seals are even known to swim on their backs for fun and relaxation.

At night, some harp seals haul out on the ice to sleep. Adults can also sleep floating just below the surface of the water, buoyed by their blubber. Every five minutes or so, a sleeping harp seal raises its head above the water, takes a breath, and sinks back below the surface without even waking up.

In ordinary dives, adult harp seals also come up for air about every 5 minutes. Since they are able to dive to a depth of 600 feet (185 m), harp seals can and do stay under water for up to 30 minutes. These amazing dives have been recorded and photographed by researchers.

Harp seals can stay under water for up to 30 minutes.

14

The harp seal's ability as a swimmer suits its migratory lifestyle. When animals **migrate**, they follow regular patterns of movement, traveling back and forth across great distances. Harp seals swim from ocean to ocean, following food trails of small fish. Some seals migrate over 3,000 miles (5,000 km) from the arctic and subarctic waters near the North Pole to the northwest Atlantic.

Swimming under the arctic ice

Harp seals spend their summers in seas along the Arctic Circle near Greenland. As winter approaches, the scattered, broken ice forms into larger, more solid masses, making northern waters a difficult and dangerous habitat for many living creatures. Arctic winter storms produce strong winds and sea currents that buckle, grind, and fracture the ice. Under normal conditions, the **pack ice** creaks and groans as it shifts, but during storms, it rumbles and roars in a frightening swell of sound. When this begins to happen, winter is definitely in charge. The fish that harp seals eat waste little time abandoning their northern waters. Except for a few stragglers, most harp seals follow their food, and start their migration southward, ahead of the pack ice. As soon as winter is over, the migration is reversed, and fish and harp seals return once more to spend summer on the fringes of the Arctic Circle near Greenland. Harp seals swim this long and dangerous route twice a year for as long as they live, which is usually 30 to 35 years.

In the distance, snow-covered pack ice has been churned up by winter storms.

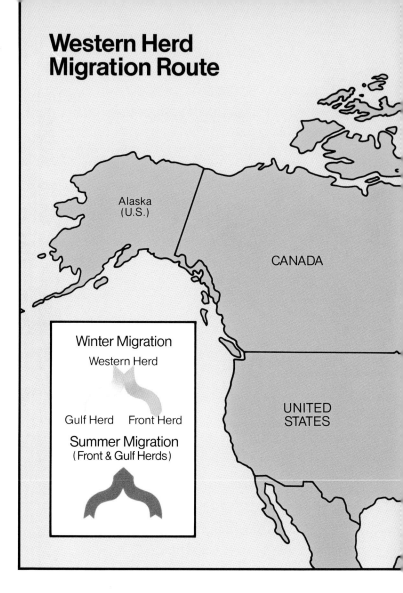

Western Herd Migration Route

Alaska (U.S.)

CANADA

UNITED STATES

Winter Migration
Western Herd

Gulf Herd   Front Herd

Summer Migration
(Front & Gulf Herds)

The harp population is made up of three distinct herds known as the Western herd, the Central herd, and the Eastern herd. The members of all three herds are the same species, yet they never mix or mate with each other. Members of one herd do not swim with, or try to be accepted by, another herd. So if one herd loses too many members and cannot produce enough pups to maintain its numbers, it will become **extinct**—the herd will die.

The Western herd begins its winter migration, leaving the coast of Greenland in October. It moves southward, keeping ahead of the advancing ice. The herd moves toward the narrow **straits**, through which it must swim before frozen pack ice locks the northern waters and cuts off its migratory route.

When the Western herd approaches the Strait of Belle Isle, it divides into the Front herd and the Gulf herd. The Front herd remains on the coasts of Labrador and Newfoundland to pup on pack ice in the "Front," as that area is called. The Gulf herd swims south and west through the Strait of Belle Isle into the Gulf of St. Lawrence, reaching pack ice near the Magdalen Islands by late February or early March, just in time

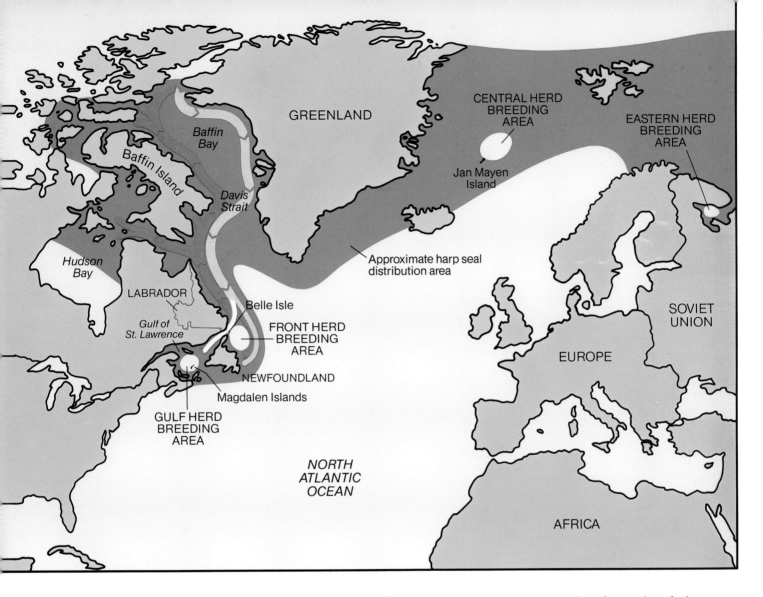

The following labels appear on the map:

GREENLAND

Baffin Bay

Baffin Island

Davis Strait

CENTRAL HERD BREEDING AREA

Jan Mayen Island

EASTERN HERD BREEDING AREA

Hudson Bay

LABRADOR

Gulf of St. Lawrence

Belle Isle

FRONT HERD BREEDING AREA

NEWFOUNDLAND

Magdalen Islands

GULF HERD BREEDING AREA

Approximate harp seal distribution area

SOVIET UNION

EUROPE

NORTH ATLANTIC OCEAN

AFRICA

for pupping. The younger members of both these herds linger along the coast of Greenland until winter conditions get much worse. Then they, too, start south, following the unmarked route of migration back to the scene of their birth. The Western herd is the only remaining large harp seal herd.

Like the Western herd, each of the two smaller herds of harp seal has its own migration route and breeding grounds. The Eastern herd migrates to Russia's White Sea to escape the arctic winter and to pup, breed, and shed, or **molt**. The Central herd migrates to the Greenland Sea near Jan Mayen Island.

Harp seals are social animals and rarely go off by themselves. They are nosy as well—and for good reason. Sensitive hairs, or whiskers, on their noses relay messages of water temperature, the nearness and movement of ice floes and air currents, the presence of food, and the activity of other seals. These whiskers serve as highly responsive feelers.

Harp seals rely on their sense of sight both under water and on land. Their eyes are large and prominent, which allows them to focus and see distinct images under water. When exposed to the glaring light on the white landscape of pack ice, their pupils narrow to a vertical slit, allowing harp seals to see fairly well on land.

A young female harp seal threatens the photographer. Notice the long whiskers, the size of the eye, and the ear opening just behind the eye.

Harp seals use their large eyes, sensitive whiskers, noses, and ears to collect the information they need to survive.

Harp seals do not have external ears as do some sea mammals. Instead they have tiny openings in the sides of their heads. When harp seals dive under water, these tiny openings close instantly to keep the water out. The delicate internal organs can receive sound waves from great distances under water. Sound waves strike the inner eardrum, informing the seal of its surroundings. These sound waves change constantly as harp seals swim and migrate. Together, the internal hearing organs, eyes, and noses of harp seals give them the wide range of information they need to survive.

Left: *The Gulf herd at the southern end of their migration route*

Below: *This harp seal has just hauled out onto the ice through an open lead. Harp seals are in danger of drowning if they get trapped under ice that is too thick to scratch through.*

The birth of the pups, breeding, and molting are the three major events in the migratory life of each herd. All three events take place when the herds are at the southern end of their migration routes.

Pups are born in late February to mid-March each year. The exact date varies and depends on the weather and the condition of the pack ice, but most of the births take place at night under the protection of darkness. Female harp seals can delay giving birth for days, if necessary, until the herd finds pack ice that is safe and sound.

The drifting ice that serves as a floating nursery is chosen carefully and with unerring instinct. The pack ice must be vast and thick enough to support many adults and pups, yet have plenty of leads and open swimming areas. As air-breathing mammals, seals sometimes have to scratch their way through fast-forming ice to open a lead for breathing, or to keep a lead open for quick escape to the comparative safety of the sea. Seals are in extreme danger of drowning if they get trapped under a frozen ceiling of solid ice too thick to scratch through.

Four harp seals peering out of leads

Harp seal about to give birth

The direction in which the ice is drifting is important to harp seals. Even in the summer, winds and currents can drive the pack ice several miles each day. Sometimes the pack ice zigzags as much as 200 miles (320 km) during the two weeks a pup lives on the frozen fields. The herd needs to find itself in a feeding area large enough to satisfy the adults, who are hungry after pupping, mating, and molting are over, and to satisfy the harp seal pups, who will eventually begin to find food for themselves.

Female harp seals pup quickly and easily, the process lasting only 15 to 40 seconds. The mother cleans and sniffs her pup and listens to its whimper. From then on she recognizes it as her own.

Left: *A mother harp seal sniffs her newborn pup, and listens to its whimper.*

Below: *Mother harp seals recognize their pups by the way they smell and sound.*

Right: *A newborn harp seal, called a yellowcoat*

Below: *A harp seal pup nurses*

At birth, a harp seal pup's fur is tinted yellow, so it is called a **yellowcoat**. It weighs about 22 pounds (10 kg) and is close to 3 feet (90 cm) long. The yellowcoat begins life with its eyes open but is entirely helpless—it cannot run and it cannot swim. It shivers on the ice, nuzzles at its mother's **teat**, and begins to **nurse** immediately.

26

Several hours after pupping, the mother harp seal dares to leave her pup temporarily to swim with the herd. She moves back and forth from the water to the ice, keeping a watchful eye on her pup. A harp seal nursery is a mass of pups, yet each mother knows exactly which one is hers. When a hungry pup nuzzles the wrong mother, she is not fooled. She promptly turns the pup away with an angry cuff. Pups do not always recognize their own mothers, and when they see a dark form that looks like her, they often approach it and expect to nurse.

A mother seal's milk is among the richest in the animal world. It is almost half butterfat and has five times as much protein as cow's milk. A harp seal pup will weigh up to 65 pounds (30 kg) by the time it is two weeks old—a gain of about 3 pounds (1.35 kg) a day!

A mother harp seal pokes through a lead to check on her pup.

About two days after birth, the yellow tint fades, leaving the pup's coat so clear and transparent that it appears to be the purest white. Although the young of some other species of seal have white fur, only the harp seal pup is called a **whitecoat**.

Right: *A thin whitecoat*

Below: *A fat whitecoat. Whitecoats can gain 3 pounds a day.*

A whitecoat under cover. The transparent white fur of a whitecoat traps heat near the surface of its skin. Because the fur also acts as a barrier between the white- coat and the freezing environment, snow around the whitecoat doesn't melt.

The transparency of the fur serves two purposes. First and most important, it lets the sun shine through to supply warmth to the whitecoat. In spite of their weight and size, newborn pups do not have a layer of blubber to keep them warm on the pack ice. So for the first two weeks of life, their transparent white coats provide needed heat and insulation while they fatten up. This self-warming ability frees the mother from the constant care of her pup. She can dive through leads and rejoin the herd for short periods of time.

The transparent fur of the whitecoat also serves a second purpose. Even though their crying can give them away, whitecoats are hard to see against the white background of the pack ice. When something other than its mother comes near, a whitecoat is at first friendly. If it is threatened, it tries to flee. When this fails, the whitecoat tucks its head under its body and "plays dead." The spotless white fur blends in perfectly with the frosty ice—it's a **camouflage** for the pups. Many thousands of pups are born and live on one square mile of pack ice. Except for their large, brown eyes, the clusters of whitecoats look like part of the landscape.

The adult harp seals are easy to see, but the four whitecoats look like part of the landscape.

A mother harp seal guides her pup away from possible danger.

"Living on thin ice" is not just a saying to the whitecoats. It is often a fact of life. Some whitecoats drown when pack ice shifts and tilts, throwing them into the sea when they are still too young to swim. Others die each year during unexpected storms that scatter and crush the ice, separating mothers from their pups. The pups and their mothers must ride the moving ice, trying to keep out of the way of danger.

When faced with danger, a mother harp seal stays with her pup as long as possible, trying to protect it and guide it to a safer, more solid area on the ice. But if the danger is great, a mother harp seal has a better chance of survival in the open water, where the males and immature females go for safety, so she abandons her pup. A whitecoat that is orphaned never survives, so the mother's care and nourishment during those first two weeks of life are vital both to the pup and to the herd.

Whitecoats sleep most of the time, and when they are not asleep, they are usually nursing. But whitecoats will occasionally crawl around—they can be curious, playful, and noisy. They waddle and wiggle and shriek for attention, or they mock and challenge each other, trying to imitate their elders. Whitecoats are constantly hungry, demanding to be fed in loud voices. Hungry pups whimper and cry, sounding very much like human babies.

When whitecoats are about two weeks old, there is a sudden and dramatic change in their lives—they are **weaned**. Mother seals no longer nurse or care for their pups. They return to the sea and the herd, leaving their pups alone on the ice. It is a terrible time for the whitecoats. They must live off their own body fat while they molt and prepare to take to the water. Because they have been fed on very rich milk, they usually have all the extra fat they need to survive this stage of growth.

Whitecoats spend most of their time eating and sleeping.

The molting process starts when a whitecoat is less than two weeks old and has developed a thick layer of blubber. At this early age, the harp pup will begin shedding its pure white fur. A growth of coarser, close-set hair slowly replaces the long silky coat. The new hair is silvery gray with black spots.

Molting is a tiresome, slow, and irritating process that lasts about one week. The whitecoats squirm and rub against jagged ice to ease the itch that comes with the changing coat. When they are partly molted and still have chunks of white fur clinging to their skins, pups are called **ragged-jackets**.

Above: *A whitecoat right before it's ready to molt. Notice the spotted gray fur that has already grown in underneath the white fur.*

Below: *Pups during their first molt are called ragged-jackets because they look so raggedy.*

Fully molted pups are called **beaters** because when they first take to the water, they are not good swimmers—they beat the water's surface. Beaters have not eaten for days and are very active, so they are much slimmer than whitecoats. Before beaters take to the water, they can move quickly on the ice. But most important to survival, the beaters' new coat of close-set hair is waterproof, and prepares them for their life in the sea.

By the time the molt is complete, instinct drives beaters to explore the surrounding water. They peer over the edge of the ice at the open sea. Finally, they crawl or fall in, and in about four weeks they learn to find and eat solid food. The fatter the pup was when it was weaned, the better its chances of survival, since blubber keeps a seal's body nourished as well as buoyant and insulated.

A molted harp seal pup, called a beater, is getting ready for its first swim.

Beaters quickly learn to swim as expertly as adult harp seals.

Once a full-fledged beater has taken to the water, it rarely goes back on the ice. Beaters keep each other company, swimming and diving along with the adults, and seeking their own food in the form of shrimplike crustaceans and small fish. Beaters apparently make no effort to renew their ties with their mothers, but seem to enjoy their free life in the sea.

At the age of one year, beaters molt and become **bedlamers**. Bedlamers live mostly on fish called capelin and plaice. Within three to seven years, bedlamers become adult harp seals and are mature enough to mate.

Above: *When harp seal pups are one year old, they molt for the second time and are called bedlamers. This bedlamer is in a threat posture.*

Right: *The spots on this female bedlamer have almost disappeared. The adult pattern, in the shape of a harp or a saddle, is beginning to appear on her back.*

A group of adult male harp seals on the pack ice

Females usually begin to breed and give birth when they are from three to five years old. Although males may start courting on the ice, mating takes place in the water and occurs shortly after the females have weaned their pups. While waiting for the females who are still nursing their pups, mature males swim excitedly to show off and attract their mates, dominating the females they court and warding off other males. They have a special call that mingles with the roaring of the herd and the shrill whimpering of hungry whitecoats. They raise their heads and send out a long, hollow "hoh," a mating call that echoes across the ice floes.

A male harp seal, searching for a mate, peers through a lead at a female.

Harp seals usually mate in the water, but occasionally they will mate on the pack ice.

Except for the 2 weeks immediately following the birth of her pup, a female harp seal is pregnant all 12 months of the year. For about 3 months after the parents mate, the **fertilized** egg remains **dormant**, or at rest, before it begins an 8- to 9-month period of growth. The developing pup must get its nutrition from the mother's body. This cycle of reproduction goes on while pregnant females migrate over long and dangerous routes with the herd, under weather conditions that are often fierce and unfriendly.

After mating is over, the adult harp seals leave the ragged-jackets behind, move to a different patch of ice, and begin to molt. Molting is as uncomfortable for adult harps as it is for the whitecoats. Harp seals are sluggish and inactive during this annual change of coat. While molting, harp seals spend most of their time sleeping on the ice.

They rub, scratch, and twitch in spasms while the old hair falls out, bit by bit.

Harp seals are neither social nor playful during the molt. But once it's over, the sea churns with thousands of vigorous, noisy seals. Then the herd moves northward, following the invisible route of migration.

Once a year, adult harp seals take to the ice to molt.

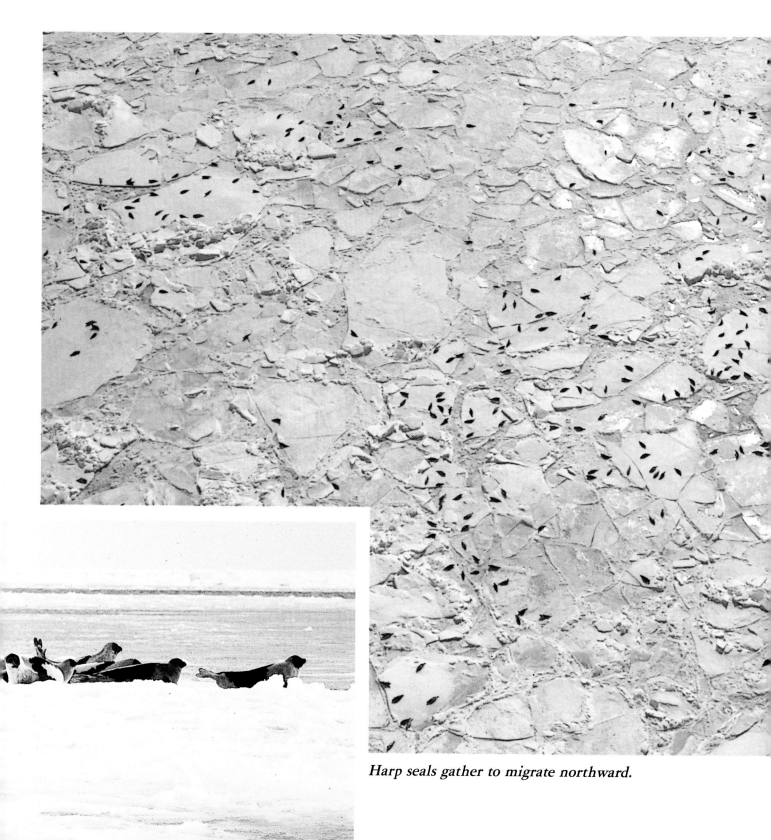

Harp seals gather to migrate northward.

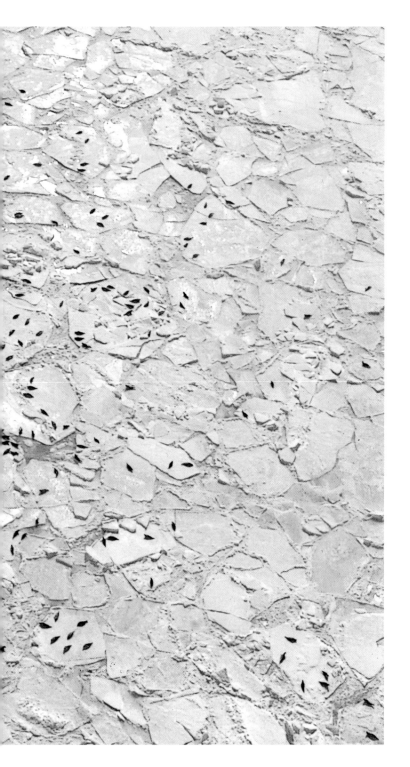

During the few weeks of pupping, mating, and molting, adult harp seals eat very little or nothing at all. A female will lose as much as 80 pounds (36 kg), about one-quarter of her body weight, during this busy season. Males lose weight, too, but much less. Both live off the nourishment of their 2-inch (5-cm) layer of blubber, just as the pups do when they are weaned. So when the migration north begins, the adults are very hungry. They dive deep into the water to feed on the abundant capelin and plaice.

After the adult herd leaves the pupping and breeding waters, beaters follow. Beaters and bedlamers swim 10 to 20 miles (16-32 km) a day at speeds of 4 to 5 mph (6.5-8.0 kph). It takes them 2½ months to go 2,000 miles (3,200 km). They find their own way by using their instincts and by relying on every bit of information they can gain from their senses. They do not become part of the main herd for a year or longer. By then, the young harp seals are almost full grown and weigh nearly as much as mature adults.

Harp seals are threatened by several natural enemies. Winter storms take their toll and kill many seals each year. Killer whales, polar bears, and sharks attack older adults that cannot swim or move fast enough to escape, and they also feed on beaters and bedlamers who are taking part in their first migration. Eskimos and other natives hunt seals for food. But the harp seal's greatest enemy has been the **sealer**. Sealers are people who commercially hunt seals in great numbers mostly for their fur skins, although they also sell the blubber.

Polar bears are one of the harp seals' natural enemies. Here, two polar bears keep watch over their dinner.

Harp seal pups are born with a luxurious white coat, so they are hunted and killed on the ice soon after birth, before they become ragged-jackets. In the past, a number of countries took part in "the hunt," as it is called. A few years ago, the hunt was televised, and the public saw for the first time what was happening on the ice. There was such an outcry against the hunt that most countries banned it and the selling of all whitecoat products, particularly the fur. In spite of the ban, hunters continue to kill whitecoats, and these people continue to be the herds' greatest enemy.

A storm is coming. The wind is rising, and floating pack ice is moving quickly. To harp seals this hostile region is home. These seals have survived centuries of arctic storms. They have developed habits and a physical form that are made to withstand the Arctic's fury. Through the advantage of their powerful bodies and the guidance of their instincts, nature guarantees the harp seal a fair chance for survival. If people act with intelligence rather than greed, every generation will have its harp seal herds to fill the arctic seas with wonder and beauty.

44

GLOSSARY

beaters: harp seal pups that have gone through their first molt, which happens when they are about three weeks old. They are called beaters until they are one year old.

bedlamers: harp seals that are at least one year old and have gone through their second molt. They remain bedlamers for at least three years, or until their adult markings appear.

blubber: a thick layer of fat, which is under the skin, that protects sea mammals from the cold

camouflage: a natural disguise that helps some animals blend into their environment, hiding them from view

dormant: temporarily inactive or at rest

extinct: not existing any longer

fertilize: to unite a male and a female reproductive cell, so that new life can develop

leads: paths of open water within the pack ice

mammals: animals, including people, who nurse their young

migrate: to move seasonally from one area to another and back again, for feeding or breeding purposes

molt: to shed, or cast off, fur or hair

nurse: to feed on mother's milk from the breast or udder

pack ice: sea ice crushed together into a widespread mass

pinnipeds: sea mammals that have flippers instead of arms and legs. Pinnipeds are members of the scientific suborder Pinnipedia.

ragged-jackets: harp seal pups that are about two weeks old, going through their first molt. They shed their white fur, exposing patches of darker and shorter hair.

sealer: a person who hunts seals

strait: a narrow path of water connecting two large bodies of water

teat: the tip of a female mammal's udder or breast, from which milk can be drawn

weaned: not allowed to nurse anymore

whitecoat: a harp seal pup, less than two weeks old, that still has its white fur

yellowcoat: a one- to three-day-old harp seal pup, whose fur has a yellowish tint

INDEX

ABOUT THE AUTHOR

Olga Cossi is a native of California and has been a free-lance writer, staff correspondent, and columnist for a variety of publications. For 11 years, Ms. Cossi lived in a converted bus, exploring Mexico and the United States from coast to coast. She has also traveled extensively in Europe. The harp seal is a subject close to Ms. Cossi's heart, and one she has been involved with for years.